# What Happens at a
# TV Station?

**By Amy Hutchings**

Reading Consultant: Susan Nations, M.Ed.,
author/literacy coach/consultant in literacy development

**WEEKLY READER**®
PUBLISHING

For a complete list of Where People Work titles,
please visit our web site at **www.garethstevens.com**.
For a free catalog describing Gareth Stevens Publishing's list of high-quality books,
call 1-800-542-2595 (USA) or 1-800-387-3178 (Canada). Our fax: 877-542-2596

**Library of Congress Cataloging-in-Publication Data**

Hutchings, Amy.
          What happens at a TV station? / by Amy Hutchings; reading consultant, Susan Nations.
                    p. cm. — (Where people work)
          Includes bibliographical references and index.
          ISBN-10: 1-4339-0070-X   ISBN-13: 978-1-4339-0070-9 (lib. bdg.)
          ISBN-10: 1-4339-0134-X   ISBN-13: 978-1-4339-0134-8 (softcover)
          1. Television broadcasting—Juvenile literature.   I. Nations, Susan.   II. Title.
     III. Title: What happens at a television station?
     PN1992.57.H88    2008
     384.55—dc22                                                         2008024999

This edition first published in 2009 by
**Weekly Reader® Books**
An Imprint of Gareth Stevens Publishing
1 Reader's Digest Road
Pleasantville, NY 10570-7000 USA

Buddy® is a registered trademark of Weekly Reader Corporation. Used under license.

Executive Managing Editor: Lisa M. Herrington
Creative Director: Lisa Donovan
Designers: Alexandria Davis, Jennifer Ryder-Talbot
Photographer: Richard Hutchings
Publisher: Keith Garton

The publisher thanks Larchmont–Mamaroneck Community Television (LMC–TV) in Mamaroneck,
New York, for its participation in the development of this book.

Printed in the United States of America

1 2 3 4 5 6 7 8 9 10 09 08

Hi, Kids!

I'm Buddy, your Weekly Reader® pal. Have you ever visited a TV station? I'm here to show and tell what happens at a TV station. So, come on. Turn the page and read along!

**Boldface** words appear in the glossary.

Lucy has a big day! She will sing in a **talent show** on TV. Lucy goes to a TV station with her dad.

First, Lucy meets the **director**. The director guides the making of a TV show.

director

The director works in the **control room**. The control room has the equipment to tape the TV show. Another worker puts the sound and pictures together.

**control room**

9

The lights in the **studio** are very bright. A worker sets up the lights before the talent show starts.

studio

Big **cameras** tape the talent show. The director talks to the workers through their headphones.

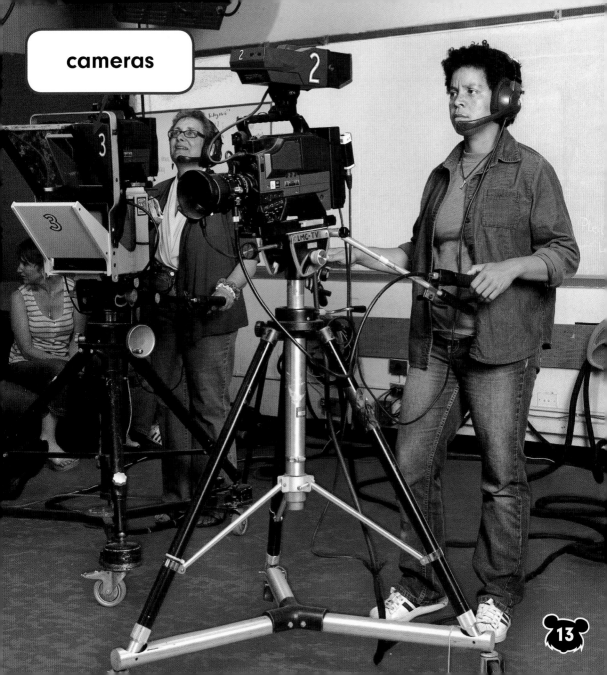

**cameras**

13

It is Lucy's turn to sing!

The **stage manager**
shows her where to go.

stage manager

15

Ready, set, action!
The cameras roll as
Lucy sings.

A worker holds a long pole. It has a **microphone** on the end. The microphone picks up Lucy's voice but cannot be seen on TV.

microphone

19

Lucy heads back to the control room. She watches herself on the tape. Being on TV is fun!

 # Glossary

**cameras:** devices that record pictures for TV

**control room:** a room that holds equipment for taping a TV show

**director:** a person who guides the making of a TV show

**microphone:** a device that makes sound louder

**stage manager:** a person in charge of what happens backstage

**studio:** a place where a TV show is made

**talent show:** a performance where people show off their talents

# For More Information

## Books

*A Day in the Life of a TV Reporter.* Jobs People Do (series). Linda Hayward (DK Publishing, 2001)

*Working at a TV Station.* Working Here (series). Gary Davis (Children's Press, 1999)

## Web Site

**Kids Work! TV Station**

*www.knowitall.org/kidswork/etv/index.html*
Meet real-life people who work at a public TV station. Follow a fun time line to learn interesting facts about the history of TV.

# Index

# About the Author

Amy Hutchings was part of the original production staff of *Sesame Street* for the first ten years of the show's history. She then went on to work with her husband, Richard, producing thousands of photographs for children's publishers. She has written several books, including *Firehouse Dog* and *Picking Apples and Pumpkins*. She lives in Rhinebeck, New York, along with many deer, squirrels, and wild turkeys.